Where Animals Live

Prairie Animals

By Katie Bu...

2 I see bison on the prairie.

I see ferrets on the prairie.

4 I see pronghorns on the prairie.

I see horses on the prairie.

I see deer on the prairie.

I see prairie chickens
on the prairie.

8 I see prairie dogs on the prairie.

I see coyotes on the prairie.

10 I see goldfinches on the prairie.

I see grasshoppers on the prairie.

I see snakes on the prairie.

I see falcons on the prairie.

Word List

vocabulary words

prairie   horses   goldfinches

bison   deer   grasshoppers

ferrets   chickens   snakes

pronghorns   dogs   falcons

              coyotes

I see bison on the prairie.

I see ferrets on the prairie.

I see pronghorns on the prairie.

I see horses on the prairie.

I see deer on the prairie.

I see prairie chickens on the prairie.

I see prairie dogs on the prairie.

I see coyotes on the prairie.

I see goldfinches on the prairie.

I see grasshoppers on the prairie.

I see snakes on the prairie.

I see falcons on the prairie.

CHERRY BLOSSOM PRESS

Published in the United States of America by Cherry Lake Publishing Group
Ann Arbor, Michigan
www.cherrylakepublishing.com

Photo Credits: © Tom Reichner/Shutterstock, cover; © Georgi Baird/Shutterstock, title page; © Tim Malek/Shutterstock, 2; © Kerry Hargrove/Shutterstock, 3; © Paul Tessier/Shutterstock, 4; © Yakov Oskanov/Shutterstock, 5; © Tom Reichner/Shutterstock, 6; © Nattapong Assalee/Shutterstock, 7; © Edwin Butter/Shutterstock, 8; © Jeff W. Jarrett/Shutterstock, 9; © Mike Truchon/Shutterstock, 10; © Gianluca Rasile/Shutterstock, 11; © Matt Jeppson/Shutterstock, 12; © JayPierstorff/Shutterstock, 13; © finchfocus/Shutterstock, 14

Note from publisher: Websites change regularly, and their future contents are outside of our control. Supervise children when conducting any recommended online searches for extended learning opportunities.

Cherry Blossom Press is an imprint of Cherry Lake Publishing Group.

Library of Congress Cataloging-in-Publication Data

Names: Buckley, Katie (Children's author), author.
Title: Prairie animals / written by Katie Buckley.
Description: Ann Arbor, Michigan : Cherry Blossom Press, [2024] | Series: Where animals live | Audience: Grades K-1 | Summary: "Prairie Animals showcases animals found in a prairie environment, including animals like bison and prairie dogs. Uses the Whole Language approach to literacy, combining sight words and repetition. Simple text makes reading these books easy and fun. Bold, colorful photographs that align directly with the text help readers with comprehension"— Provided by publisher.
Identifiers: LCCN 2023035091 | ISBN 9781668937617 (paperback) | ISBN 9781668939994 (ebook) | ISBN 9781668941348 (pdf)
Subjects: LCSH: Prairie animals—Juvenile literature. | Prairie ecology—Juvenile literature.
Classification: LCC QL115.3 .B83 2024 | DDC 591.74/4—dc23/eng/20230905
LC record available at https://lccn.loc.gov/2023035091

Printed in the United States of America

Katie Buckley grew up in Michigan and continues to call the Mitten her home. When she's not writing and editing, you'll find her gardening, playing music, and spending time with her dog, Scout. She has always loved books and animals, so she's a big fan of this series.